The Infinite Money Tree

Kyla Lovell

DISCLAIMER: Educational and Entertainment Purposes Only

This book is written solely for educational and entertainment purposes and is in no way intended to substitute for professional financial or legal advice. Do not misconstrue the content of this book as expert guidance or as an alternative to personalized advice from a certified financial planner or advisor.

The author and publisher absolve themselves of any liability or responsibility for any direct or indirect loss, mishaps, or consequential damages that may occur as a result of the usage or implementation of the information provided in this book.

Remember, every person's financial situation is unique, and thus, the strategies and concepts discussed in this book may not suit or benefit everyone. Therefore, it's emphatically recommended that individuals seek custom advice from qualified professionals to address their particular financial needs and concerns. This book is not a replacement for such advice and should be used as a starting point for understanding the topics discussed.

Table of Contents

Contents

Acknowledgements 5
Foreword 6
Introduction 7
Let's Start with the Problem 9
1 — The Solution | Welcome to Infinite Banking 12
    The Origins and Development of Infinite Banking 15
    How Infinite Banking Work 18
    Advantages — Tax Perks 21
2— Life insurance 32
    The Permanent vs. Term Life Insurance Showdown 32
    Term-Life Insurance (The Temporary Lifeline) 33
    Permanent Life Insurance 35
    Permanent Life Insurance Types 36
    Other Permanent Life Insurance Options 37
3 — Infinite Banking Goal Today 39
    About IBC and Whole Life Insurance 43
4— Infinite Banking Structure 44
    Non-direct Vs. Direct Recognition Life Insurance 46
5 — Double Your Cash or Surrender 48
    Reasons for Surrendering a Life Insurance Policy 49
    Cost of Surrendering a Life Insurance Policy 49
    Surrender Options 50
6 — Application of the Infinite Banking Concept 56

    Economic Crises and Infinite Banking 5

    Infinite Banking Concept–A Safe Financial Harbor 6

7— Cash Value 6

    What's Cash Value, Anyway? 6

    How Cash Value Works 6

    Cash Value in Action 6

    Your Own Personal Banking System 6

8— Is Infinite Banking a Reality? 6

9 — Final Word 7

    Curious? Want more information? Ready to get started? 7

Resources 7

NOTES 7

Acknowledgements

In loving memory of Gloria Blair, my grandmother who started me on the path of leaving a financial legacy.

I'm extremely grateful for the successful completion of my dissertation, which would not have been possible without the support and nurturing of so many wonderful people.

I cannot begin to express my thanks to my three children, Amun, Nai, and Zay, who gave me a reason to persevere and inspired me every day. To their father, thank you for allowing me the time and space to focus on this work.

I must also thank my mother for instilling in me a love of books and reading, and my father for always telling me that I can do anything I set my mind to. My aunts, your unwavering support has been my solid foundation. To my friends, thank you for being an escape from reality and a constant source of joy.

I would like to extend my sincere thanks to David Strauss, my editor, for his invaluable contributions, and to Silas Goja for his exceptional work in research and development. Your efforts have been instrumental in bringing this dissertation to completion.

Special thanks to my whole team who did all the behind-the-scenes work.

Foreword

Ready to take control of your financial destiny and achieve true financial freedom?
One method many people use is a concept called "infinite banking". Developed originally by Nelson Nash in his book "Becoming Your Own Banker: The Infinite Banking Concept," which outlined how you can borrow from yourself utilizing the cash value of your whole life insurance.

The Infinite Money Tree by Kyla Lovell, is a valuable resource in understanding and applying this concept for your own personal financial plan. She simplifies infinite banking, by breaking it down into bite-sized, easily digestible pieces.
You will get an in-depth education of the various Life insurance plans and options that are available and how they can play a role in infinite banking. She also reveals the pros and cons for you to consider. And while she cautions that this is a strategy for building long-term wealth that requires patience and diligence, she also highlights the great benefits that it can help you achieve in accelerating your wealth.

To your financial success,

Sharon Lechter

www.sharonlechter.com

Author of *Think and Grow Rich for Women*, Co-author of *How Money Works for Women, Exit Rich, Outwitting the Devil, Three Feet from Gold, Rich Dad Poor Dad* and 14 other Rich Dad books.

Introduction

Growing Your Infinite Money Tree for Life's Major Milestones

Are you confident about your retirement planning? If you are balancing the ever- rising cost of living while planning for your future, you will find this book helpful.

You may be holding the key to your financial challenges, but you are unaware. Rather than trying to balance the tight financial situation, what if you find a reliable income source that will guarantee you financial security through retirement and offer you liquidity for significant life events like handling massive purchases, starting a business, or raising children. Imagine the security and peace of mind you will experience knowing that you are financially secure throughout your life.

I am a mother of three young children, and I know how important it is to be financially stable. We look forward to a financially secure future, quality time with our loved ones, and a peaceful retirement. Also, some of us desire to start new businesses or expand existing ones and turn them into successful ventures that meet our needs and enhance our financial security. The Infinite Banking Concept through whole life insurance is a strategy that has been tried, tested, and found to meet these goals. Therefore, I'm overjoyed to uncover this secret for you in "The Infinite Money Tree."

Take a moment to think about a magical tree that keeps providing for your entire family, offering abundance throughout the years. This can only be actualized by the Infinite Banking Concept. If you plant the money tree seed that keeps growing your entire life, you secure a guaranteed financial security that will safeguard you and your whole generation.

The concept of infinite banking can be applied to our unique circumstances, be it parents, retirees, or entrepreneurs. This strategy enables you to utilize your life insurance's cash value as a financial tool, allowing you to easily access your funds for various purposes, such as running a business, raising kids, managing significant purchases, and planning for retirement.

This book highlights the principles of the infinite banking concept, uncovering the secrets to taking full advantage of its potential to turn around and rejuvenate your financial future. We break down whole life insurance policies, which act as the backbone of this strategy, and offer an illustration of how you can enjoy the full benefits of this strategy if properly designed for your situation. You will find practical examples to help you understand how powerful this approach can be for your retirement planning, business, and family.

If you want financial stability, join me on this journey.

Let's Start with the Problem

When discussing money, many people find themselves in a familiar predicament: they don't have enough funds to meet their needs, often resorting to bank loans or personal credit to bridge the income gap. While this can provide a temporary fix, it's not a viable long-term solution.

Banks tend to charge exorbitant interest rates, which can eat away at future earnings, ultimately benefiting the banks more than their customers. Borrowing money to sustain your lifestyle or to cover financial gaps robs you of your future earnings, making it difficult to save for retirement or plan for unexpected expenses.

Many people hesitate to seek personal loans from banks due to high-interest rates, strict lending requirements, and the possibility of needing to provide collateral as security. These factors raise concerns and act as red flags for people reluctant to entrust their hard-earned money to a bank, especially considering the potential consequences if they cannot repay the debt. The core issue with banks is straightforward: repaying a loan entails paying interest. If someone is already struggling financially, repaying the bank with interest becomes a significant burden, potentially leading to added distress down the road.

Finding peace of mind regarding the security of your money, regardless of the investment choice, is not easy. Even depositing money in a traditional bank carries risks, as banks collapse, particularly those without government insurance coverage, can wreak unexpected havoc on your finances. Recent collapses of several large banks in the United States have instilled widespread fear and uncertainty among their depositors.

One significant problem is the need for more awareness regarding alternative financial tools beyond bank loans or personal credit that can help bridge income gaps. Life insurance is a powerful financial tool in this regard, yet it needs to be more widely understood and utilized. Surprisingly, only 20% of people choose to invest in life insurance. This low percentage can be attributed to a lack of awareness regarding the power and potential of life insurance as a vital component for retirement and financial and retirement planning.

The most common understanding of life insurance is that its sole purpose is to provide a death benefit, meaning its value is realized by beneficiaries when the insured person passes away. However, there are hybrid policies that can be strategically designed to serve as a financial safety net during challenging times. These include premature death, retirement, or poor investment decisions that impact the family breadwinner.

While the traditional death benefit is straightforward, what about navigating the consequences of poor financial choices? We all make mistakes, especially when it comes to investing. Maybe we trusted a friend's new business idea without realizing the risks. Or we dabbled in the stock market without the necessary knowledge or expertise. Even diving into real estate without understanding property values and market trends can lead to regrets. Another common error is relying solely on internet searches, social media influencers, or TV financial hosts instead of seeking professional advice to understand the risks of an investment. A carefully selected insurance policy can serve as a valuable safety net in each of these situations.

When planning for retirement, there are plenty of investment options to consider. If your top priority is steady growth with minimal risk, you might discover that the infinite banking concept offers your best choice for growth, security, and peace of mind.

At first, many people may have reservations about withdrawing their life savings from a bank and investing it in an insurance product under the infinite banking concept; however, as they delve deeper into understanding how infinite banking functions, these concerns gradually dissipate. They realize that infinite banking can be the most sensible and secure choice for their financial planning.

This realization marks the start of the Infinite Banking Concept, which empowers you to become your own banker. Through this approach, life insurance policies can be utilized to earn bonuses and access funds through loans against the accumulated growth in the policy's cash value. This method bypasses the challenges typically associated with obtaining loans from banks or other financial services for investment purposes.

1 — The Solution | Welcome to Infinite Banking

If you are one of the millions of people tired of dealing with the frustrations and high interest rates that come with traditional banking and personal credit, what if you could break free from this cycle and take control of your financial future? Welcome to the world of infinite banking, where possibilities abound, and financial freedom becomes a reality.

Infinite banking is a powerful tool that allows you to use the cash value of a whole life insurance policy as a pool of money from which you can borrow, eliminating the need to rely on traditional banks for loans or credit. It's like having your own private water reservoir instead of depending on the city's water supply. Just as a reservoir collects rainwater over time, providing a constant supply for your household needs, with infinite banking, you invest in a whole life insurance policy that accumulates cash value through regular premium payments. This cash value can be borrowed against for personal needs or major expenses.

In contrast, relying on city water is similar to using a traditional bank. You have no control over the supply or the rates set by the city, and the costs can increase over time. Similarly, taking loans from a bank means being subject to their terms, high interest rates, and control over the loan process.

Having your own water reservoir gives you control over your water supply. You can use it whenever you want, without any additional costs. Similarly, having cash value in a whole life insurance policy allows you to borrow against it when you need to, set your repayment terms, and any interest you pay goes back into your policy, not to a bank.

Managing your whole life policy properly by paying your monthly premiums keeps it in force and allows it to continue to grow, just like managing your private water reservoir to ensure a constant water supply.

Let's discuss the problem with traditional bank loans. Securing a loan from a bank can often feel like navigating a tricky obstacle course. While many people manage to get the loan they requested, the obligation to pay it back with hefty interest becomes a significant burden. It's like climbing a mountain, with each step accumulating more weight on your back. The loan becomes an additional burden, making the climb steeper and more challenging. The interest on the loan acts as extra weight, weighing you down and making it harder to achieve your financial goals.

However, there's an alternative pathway that allows you to avoid these challenging conditions: the Infinite Banking Concept (IBC). Think of it as finding a secret passage that takes you to your destination faster and with fewer obstacles. Just like finding a hidden tunnel through a mountain, the IBC enables you to become your own banker by leveraging the cash within your insurance policy. It's like having a personal guide who knows all the secret routes and helps you navigate the financial landscape more efficiently.

Feeling overwhelmed by this new concept? Don't worry; it's natural when exploring new territory. Just as an experienced mountaineer or guide can assist you in conquering the mountain, the concept of infinite banking can be your financial lifesaver.

So, what exactly is infinite banking? At its core, infinite banking empowers you to use your life insurance policy as collateral for loans. It's like having a valuable asset, such as a climbing rope, that supports and secures your financial journey. Whether you need funds for potential investments, daily expenses, or the cost of education for your kids, infinite banking offers a more convenient alternative to traditional banks. The key advantage lies in the fact that the funds are already available within your insurance policy, just waiting to be utilized.

Now, let's dive into the origins of this concept. Just as a mountain guide has years of experience and knowledge, infinite banking has its own story and driving force. Let's delve into the tale behind infinite banking and discover the vision that led to its development.

The concept of infinite banking was introduced by Nelson Nash, the pioneer of the Infinite Banking Concept (IBC). He presented a straightforward process where the cash value of money in a life insurance policy guarantees the loan. Compared to traditional banking, IBC offers a simpler approach. To implement this concept, you only need to contact your insurance agent and request a policy loan, which is a basic aspect of life insurance.

The value of life insurance tends to increase over time. For example, if someone has secured a life insurance policy worth $1 million, it can potentially multiply and reach over $5 million by the time of their death. When the time comes to access and utilize the funds, withdrawing the money in the form of a loan is easily achievable.

The infinite banking concept, as coined by Nelson Nash in his book "Becoming Your Own Banker: The Infinite Banking Concept," revolutionizes the way people manage their finances. Imagine having the power to be your own banker, setting your own terms and conditions for utilizing your assets in the future. This concept has proven beneficial to many people because it provides an alternative to traditional bank loans.

To understand the concept, let's consider an example. Imagine you have a life insurance policy that has accumulated a significant cash value over the years. Instead of approaching a bank for a loan, you have the opportunity to use your life insurance policy as collateral. Whether you need funds for a potential investment, daily expenses, or education fees, the infinite banking concept offers a more convenient and flexible solution. The best part is that the money is already within your insurance policy, waiting to be utilized.

You might be curious about the origins of this innovative concept and how Nelson Nash, the creator, came up with such a unique idea. Nelson Nash, an insurance broker with an impressive 47 years of experience, had a distinct perspective. It was through his interactions with clients that he stumbled upon a fascinating pattern. He noticed that most people perceived life insurance solely as a means for their families to benefit after their passing. However, they were unaware of the potential to utilize the cash value within their life insurance policy to benefit their families while they were still alive. This realization had a profound impact on Nash, leading him to conclude that "Your need for finance during your lifetime is greater than your need for death protection."

The Origins and Development of Infinite Banking

As we wander down the path of infinite banking, we've had many conversations about the headaches and hurdles that come with traditional banks. Now, what if I told you that Nelson Nash, the mastermind behind infinite banking, went through these same struggles? It was those issues that got him thinking about a different way of banking.

Now, to really get a grasp on the seeds of infinite banking, we need to take a trip back in time. Picture this: The Great Depression was kicked off by the 1929 stock market crash that sent tremors through the world of finance, leading to the downfall of countless banks. During this turbulent time, there were whispers that banks and other financial institutions weren't getting all their dues, but insurance companies were holding up pretty well. This tidbit caught Nash's ear and led him to join forces with Citigroup to peel back the layers of this mystery and shine a light on the 1930s' financial scene. Joining the mission, Huerta and Silverman (H&S) decided to lend a hand to Nash, digging into the situation and pulling together some data to pit the performance of banks against the insurance sector.

What they found reinforced Nash's hunch – the insurance sector had indeed done better than banks. H&S published a statement showing a steady rise in both the insurance and banking industries throughout the 1920s, which lent weight to Nash's point of view. It underlined the insurance sector's strong position in the ring with banks. The statement pointed out that the annual income of banks had grown by 4.5%, from $43.7 billion in 1921 to $62.4 billion in 1929.

But here's the kicker - the life insurance industry had an even more impressive run, showing an annual growth of 10.4% from $7.9 billion in 1921 to $17.5 billion in 1929. By the close of 1929, the total value of life insurance policies had shot up from $43.9 billion to $102.1 billion. Not to mention, the assets of the life insurance sector surged at a rate twice that of banks in the same time frame. By the end of 1929, there were a whopping 123 million life insurance policies in place, quite an achievement considering the tough times.

These numbers go to show just how deep an impact life insurance policy had on people's lives - a trend that continued with Nash's introduction of infinite banking. During the Great Depression, as banks struggled and people had a hard time getting their hands on their savings, life insurance companies stepped up, playing a critical role in shielding their customers' assets. While the depression did hit the insurance sector too, it didn't hit as hard as it did the banks. While banks saw a 38% fall, life insurance companies faced only about a 14% drop.

Insurance brokers noticed that their clients stuck by them through the Great Depression, trusting in the steady and reliable nature of the insurance sector. By parking their assets with insurance companies, policyholders could keep their investments safe and sound. This experience transformed Nash's view on insurance carriers, opening his eyes to the potential they held for more than just providing financial cover to beneficiaries after their death.

Nash dreamed of a world where people could tap into and make use of their assets while they're still alive, enabling them to create returns for themselves and their family. This dream led to the birth of infinite banking, offering a lifeline to those who were left high and dry by traditional banks. But, even with its potential perks, many still don't know about or are unsure about the concept of infinite banking.

Flash forward to the 1980s, and Nelson Nash, a financial expert and advocate of the Austrian School of Economics, brought the idea of infinite banking to the world. Nash spread the word about this idea through his book, "Becoming Your Own Banker". The Austrian School of Economics, founded by Carl Menger in 1871, broke the mold of classical economic theory back then. It introduced a novel view called the "Subjective Theory of Value," tying value to scarcity and utility, rather than just how much labor or resources went into something.

Economists like Friedrich Hayek, Murray Rothbard, and Ludwig von Mises embraced the Austrian School of Economics. Inspired by this school of thought, Nash devised the strategy of people becoming their own personal bankers to meet their individual financial goals, without having to depend on the traditional banking system solely.

Now, let's go on to how the infinite banking system works and take a look at the pivotal role your whole life insurance policy plays in this scheme.

How Infinite Banking Work

Infinite banking can sound a bit daunting, but when you break it down, it's actually pretty simple. It's like unlocking a personal bank within your whole life insurance policy. You get all sorts of perks - think tax benefits, decent interest rates, and the freedom to spend your money as you see fit. The aim is to take back control of your financial life and say goodbye to traditional banks. Here's how it works:

Borrowing Tax-Free:

One of the best parts of infinite banking is that you can borrow against your life insurance policy's cash value and not have to worry about tax implications. Say you've accumulated $100,000 in cash value in your policy. Rather than heading to a bank for a loan, you can borrow some of that cash value from your insurance policy. The awesome part is, the money you borrow doesn't count as taxable income.

Growing Your Cash Value:

As a whole life insurance policyholder, your policy's cash value grows tax-free over time. This cash value is the foundation of your infinite banking strategy. If you've been religiously paying your premiums for a good few years, that cash value can grow significantly. This growing cash value is tax-deferred, meaning it's a valuable asset for your future financial needs.

Overfunding Your Life Insurance:

The secret sauce of the infinite banking strategy is pumping in more than the basic premium into your life insurance policy with after-tax money. Doing these speeds up your policy's cash value growth. Any extra premium you put in goes directly into the cash value, allowing it to grow faster. With a bigger cash value, you can borrow more money for whatever you need. Overfunding not only boosts your borrowing power, but it also increases your potential for long-term wealth accumulation.

Like a traditional banking system, infinite banking lets you loan money to yourself using your policy's cash value. While you use the borrowed money for expenses like tuition fees or medical bills, your whole life insurance policy continues to earn dividends.

Remember, infinite banking is a marathon, not a sprint. It's meant to act like your personal savings account, allowing your money to grow steadily over time. The cash in your policy is guaranteed not to decrease in value, and you can access it whenever you want without worrying about taxes.

Infinite banking gives you the key to financial independence and the power to shape your own financial future. You become your own banker, using the benefits of whole life insurance to secure your financial tomorrow.

So, let's talk about how whole life insurance plays into the infinite banking concept.

In this case study, we wanted to show how using a whole life insurance policy in the Infinite Banking Concept can offer some serious long-term benefits. By consistently paying premiums, the policy's cash value grew over time, eventually surpassing the total amount deposited.

As the policy matured, the accumulated cash value provided a safety net for the future. It could be used for college expenses, starting a business, or any other financial needs. On top of this, the policy continued to provide a death benefit, ensuring a tax-free sum for the beneficiaries if anything happened to the policyholder.

The "Baby Smith Policy" case study illustrates the power of whole life insurance in the Infinite Banking Concept. It highlights how the cash value can grow and how it can be used for future financial plans. By using this concept, you can create a reliable, self-sustaining financial system that offers control, flexibility, and long-term wealth accumulation.

Bear in mind, everyone's financial situation is different, and it's crucial to talk with a qualified financial professional who can help you navigate the Infinite Banking Concept and choose the best insurance policy for your needs and goals.

				NON-GUARANTEED			
AGE	YR	POLICY PREMIUM	DIVIDEND	DIV OPT	PREMIUM OUTLAY	CASH VALUE	DEATH BENEFIT	MAXIMUM PAID-UP INSURANCE
1	1	2,400	128	PUA	2,400	128	258,451	2,026
2	2	2,400	154	PUA	2,400	286	260,809	4,384
3	3	2,400	175	PUA	2,400	2,446	263,403	36,212
4	4	2,400	197	PUA	2,400	5,227	266,218	74,687
5	5	2,400	219	PUA	2,400	8,159	269,240	112,410
6	6	2,400	245	PUA	2,400	11,233	272,492	149,201
7	7	2,400	269	PUA	2,400	14,450	275,931	185,038
8	8	2,400	296	PUA	2,400	17,823	279,579	220,007
9	9	2,400	321	PUA	2,400	21,357	283,395	254,134
10	10	2,400	347	PUA	2,400	25,056	287,371	287,371

Source: Wealth Creation

In this case study, when their kid hit her sweet sixteen, the parents thought buying her a car would be a good idea. So, they decided to take out a loan a g a i n s t their whole life insurance policy. Over the next five years, they managed to pay off the loan, but the policy kept growing. This example shows how the parents, and later their daughter when she became an adult and took over the policy, used the Infinite Banking Concept (IBC) to buy a car and a house.

Let's dive deeper into the world of infinite banking, exploring its pros and cons. That way, you'll be able to make informed decisions and figure out how to make the best use of this concept, along with a whole life insurance policy that suits your needs and your family's needs.

Advantages — Tax Perks

One of the greatest things about the Infinite Banking Concept is its hefty tax benefits, making your money work harder for you. When you purchase a whole life insurance policy, you can access several tax benefits. Here's how three of these could benefit you.

Death Benefit:

This is usually tax-free and goes straight to your beneficiaries when you pass away. They receive the entire death benefit without having to worry about tax deductions. If your estate is likely to be taxed, you can use the death benefit to cover these taxes rather than having them deducted from your estate's cash or equity.

Growth: The cash value of your whole life insurance policy grows tax-deferred, which means you only pay taxes on the growth when you decide to withdraw or surrender the policy. This allows your cash value to grow uninterrupted by immediate tax obligations.

Policy Loans:

This is another major perk of the infinite banking concept. You see when you borrow against the cash value of your policy, you don't trigger immediate taxes. So if you take out a policy loan to buy a new car, it's not considered a taxable event because it's a loan against the cash, not a withdrawal. If you were to withdraw cash, like you would from a savings account, you'd probably trigger a taxable event. So, this neat little trick of borrowing instead of withdrawing is a handy, tax-efficient way to access your policy's value.

Also, any dividends you get as a policyholder are usually not taxable. These dividends help grow your policy's cash value, increasing its overall worth without triggering immediate tax liabilities.

Compared to traditional banking, infinite banking offers unique tax benefits that you usually don't get with conventional banks. This can lead to a more favorable tax scenario, making infinite banking a very attractive financial strategy.

It's worth noting t h o u g h, that tax laws and regulations can differ by location, and your unique circumstances can affect your tax outcomes. So, make sure you talk to a qualified tax professional or financial advisor who can provide personalized advice based on your situation.

Leverage:

The cash value of a whole life insurance policy gives policyholders a chance to take out loans or lines of credit, offering financial flexibility and the ability to invest or make purchases. This is a really handy feature of the infinite banking concept.

The death benefit provided by a whole life insurance policy can also be quite valuable, especially if you were to pass away prematurely. It's a safety net for your beneficiaries, ensuring they're financially protected. Plus, it's a comfort knowing that your loved ones will receive a significant payout.

One of the best things about the death benefit is that it's available from the get- go. From the moment you take out the policy, you get immediate value for every dollar you put in. You don't have to wait for the death benefit to accumulate over time like you would with other assets like Registered Retirement Savings Plan (RRSP) and the Tax-Free Savings Account (TFSA).

In the case of RRSPs or TFSA, if you pass away with money in those accounts, your beneficiaries still get the funds, but they'd be taxed as ordinary income. This means they could lose a big chunk of the money to taxes, and the final amount they receive could be significantly less.

With whole life insurance, the death benefit isn't taxed. The full amount is paid out to your loved ones, providing them with a hefty sum that isn't subject to any taxation. This can be a huge advantage, ensuring your beneficiaries get the full value of the death benefit without any tax deductions.

By using the infinite banking concept and incorporating whole life insurance into your financial strategy, you can provide your family with a guaranteed, tax-free death benefit. It offers them financial security and gives them peace of mind.

Guarantees

Whole life insurance policies are well-known for their guarantees. They give policyholders peace of mind and predictable outcomes. When set up correctly, these policies offer a bunch of really impressive guarantees. Let's look at four key guarantees you'll often find in whole life insurance policies, using Guardian Life as an example:

Guaranteed Endowment:

With this guarantee, if the insured individual reaches a specified age (typically 100 or 121), there is assurance that the death benefit will be paid out, even if the policyholder is still alive. This guarantee ensures that the policyholder can benefit from the policy's death benefit during their lifetime.

Guaranteed Cash Value:

A whole life insurance policy comes with a guarantee of cash value growth at a predetermined annual rate. The cash value is designed to reach the face policy amount at a specified age (usually 100 or 121). This guarantee provides policyholders with a reliable and predictable accumulation of cash value over the life of the policy.

Guaranteed Death Benefit:

The whole life insurance policy guarantees that the death benefit, the sum of money passed on to beneficiaries, will never decrease. Regardless of market fluctuations or policy performance, the agreed-upon amount is assured. This guarantee ensures that your loved ones will receive the intended financial protection, offering stability and peace of mind.

Guaranteed Level Premium: As long as you continue to pay your premiums, the whole life insurance policy will remain in effect. The premium amount remains constant and does not increase over time. This guarantee provides policyholders with stability and predictability in terms of their ongoing premium payments.

It's important to note that while some whole life insurance policies can earn dividends, dividend payments are not guaranteed. It is recommended to research and select insurance companies known for consistently paying dividends. Owning a dividend-paying whole life insurance policy allows policyholders to leverage its potential within the Infinite Banking Concept (IBC) system, enhancing the overall benefits and potential returns.

Combining these guarantees and the potential for dividend payments makes whole life insurance an attractive option for establishing and utilizing an IBC system. These guarantees ensure policyholders have a reliable and secure financial instrument that aligns with their long-term goals and provides a strong foundation for implementing the Infinite Banking Concept.

Cash Flow and Liquidity

Policyholders can experience the benefits of consistent cash flow and liquidity by accessing the cash value of their whole life insurance policy to meet various financial needs or to take advantage of attractive opportunities that require cash. Whole life insurance serves as a non-correlated asset within an investment portfolio, offering potential stability and diversification.

One of the key advantages of the infinite banking concept is the control it grants to policyholders. They have authority over the cash value, investment decisions, and the utilization of funds, empowering them with greater financial autonomy.

By leveraging a whole life insurance policy within the infinite banking concept, people can enhance their liquidity and cash flow. Unlike other assets like bonds, stocks, or real estate, whole life insurance stands out as a highly liquid asset. It provides immediate access to funds without the bureaucratic processes often associated with traditional banks. Policyholders can simply request a policy loan from their insurer and receive the cash they need. Alternatively, they can choose to withdraw funds from their whole life insurance policy.

Opting for a policy loan allows policyholders to benefit from uninterrupted compound interest, maximizing the growth potential of their policy's cash value. However, withdrawing funds may impact the accumulation of compound interest. Nonetheless, due to the liquidity of whole life insurance, it acts as a vital component of one's financial foundation, serving as a reliable source of emergency savings.

During unforeseen circumstances such as job loss, expensive home repairs, or medical bills, policyholders can borrow money from their whole life insurance policy to cover these unexpected expenses. They can even receive income to address emerging needs.

An illustrative example of the infinite banking concept through a whole life insurance policy involves Tom. Let's say Tom owns a car worth $20,000 with 100% equity, which typically signifies being debt-free. However, if Tom also owes $20,000 on the same car while simultaneously having $20,000 in his life insurance policy, earning tax-deferred compound interest, would he still be considered debt-free? Strictly speaking, Tom would have a debt of $20,000. However, he would also possess $20,000 in liquid cash available whenever he needs it. Consequently, Tom's overall balance sheet would reflect an overall debt of zero.

This example demonstrates how the infinite banking concept, implemented through a whole life insurance policy, enables people to effectively utilize their assets, maintain liquidity, and exercise greater control over their financial affairs.

Non-Correlated Asset

Think of a non-correlated asset as the sturdy oak tree in your investment garden that doesn't sway with the breeze of the stock market or other traditional investments. Whole life insurance could be that oak tree for you. It's worth noting that it's not ideal to have all of your investment trees be oaks; a diverse mix of trees would make your garden more resilient. But having an oak tree-like whole life insurance introduces a level of stability and provides shelter from the whims of the market.

The charm of whole life insurance as a non-correlated asset is its ability to promise steady and assured yearly growth in cash value. The growth of cash within the policy doesn't dance to the stock market's tune. Therefore, whole life insurance offers a rock-steady path to managing your finances, no matter the market's mood.

By planting a non-correlated asset like whole life insurance in your investment garden, you can potentially buffer some of the risks tied to market storms. This can result in a more balanced and diverse approach to nurturing your wealth. It's crucial to review your individual financial goals and aspirations to decide the best place to plant your non-correlated assets within your investment garden.

Remember that diversity is the lifeblood of a healthy investment garden. By including plants with different growth and yield patterns, like whole life insurance, you can potentially temper the overall unpredictability of your garden. However, it's always wise to seek the counsel of a seasoned financial gardener who can offer tailored guidance based on your specific financial climate and growth objectives.

Control

The infinite banking concept hands you the reins over your financial assets through your whole life insurance policy, effectively turning you into your own personal banker. When you borrow funds from your policy for personal, business, or family needs, it's like setting your own interest rate.

A key part of this control is the tax-deferred nature of the cash value tucked away in your policy. When you take out a loan against this cash value, it keeps blooming within the policy itself. Picture it this way: imagine you borrow $50,000 from your insurance company, using your cash value as collateral. But this cash value stays put within the policy, continuing to accumulate interest and possibly dividends.

So, while you're spending your cash value elsewhere, your policy keeps piling up compound interest, essentially making your money pull double duty. It's as if your money has mastered the art of being in two places at once! This exclusive feature lets your financial assets keep sprouting through your policy over your lifetime.

By holding this level of control, you can strategically use the cash value of your policy to meet your financial needs, all while soaking up the growth potential of your policy. This control empowers you to tweak your financial strategy to its optimum, potentially boosting your wealth and securing a comfortable financial future.

Bear in mind employing the infinite banking concept calls for careful thought and a firm grasp of your unique financial aims and circumstances. Teaming up with a savvy financial advisor can guide you through the twists and turns of this strategy, tailoring it to your personal needs.

Just like any strategy, the infinite banking concept comes with its own set of drawbacks and aspects to think about. Here are some of the cons tied to the infinite banking concept:

Lack of Diversification

The idea's main focus is to use a whole life insurance policy. This means your assets are collected in one spot, which might lead to a lack of diversification. Depending entirely on a whole life insurance policy for wealth growth could restrict your access to different market prospects and asset types.

Eligibility Requirements

The first step to applying the infinite banking system is qualifying for a whole life insurance policy. If you don't pass the necessary requirements, like a medical exam, it might not be possible to use the infinite banking concept effectively. Factors such as health conditions and life expectancy determine eligibility and premium rates.

Policy Cost

Whole life insurance usually comes with higher premiums compared to other types of life insurance like term life insurance. The elevated costs linked with whole life insurance could put a strain on your finances and need careful budgeting. It's crucial to gauge whether the potential benefits outweigh the financial impact of the premiums and fit in with your long-term financial goals.

Discipline and Perspective

Applying the infinite banking concept needs discipline and a particular mindset. It includes actively handling the policy, making loan repayments, and balancing the growth of the cash value with other financial responsibilities. Without the necessary discipline and long-term view, the benefits of the infinite banking concept might not be fully harnessed.

It's important to recognize that the infinite banking concept isn't a traditional or straightforward way of financing. However, it opens the door for personal growth, mindset evolution, and financial progression. Embracing the role of being an "honest banker" means taking charge of your financial future, setting clear goals, and practicing self-honesty.

Discipline is central to the infinite banking concept. Failing to repay your policy loan, except when using it for retirement, can impede your wealth growth. Therefore, maintaining discipline in managing your finances is crucial for long- term success.

Remember, the infinite banking concept is not a shortcut to immediate rewards; it's a long-term wealth-building strategy that takes time and patience.

Weighing both the pros and cons, it's clear that implementing the infinite banking concept calls for extensive research, professional guidance, and consultation with your insurance agent. It's vital to make informed decisions and adapt the concept to fit your unique financial circumstances and objectives.

Finally, looking back at the context of the Great Depression and its aftermath, it's clear that life insurance played a critical role in providing stability and financial aid during tough times. Life insurance proved to be a valuable asset during economic upheaval, paving the way for the development of the self-banking concept that helped people bounce back from the impacts of the Great Depression. This historical context highlights the resilience of life insurance and its importance in providing support during challenging periods.

2— Life insurance

Life is full of surprises. We never know when our time on this big, beautiful rock will end, and thinking about how our loved ones will cope once we're gone can feel pretty daunting. Many of us try to prepare in our own ways — whether stashing some cash away for a rainy day or ticking off those bucket list adventures one by one. At the end of the day, we want to ensure our family is taken care of when we've shuffled off this mortal coil. But, you know, there's one thing a bunch of folks often overlook: life insurance.

Finding the perfect life insurance policy can feel like hunting for a needle in a haystack, which leads to the million-dollar question: What's the best life insurance to keep your hard-earned money safe? Should you hitch your wagon to permanent life insurance or term life insurance? We've touched on these options before, but let's roll up our sleeves and dig a little deeper into what they're all about.

The Permanent vs. Term Life Insurance Showdown

Choosing between permanent and term life insurance can be as baffling as a hedge maze. If you're part of the crowd who finds it tough to tell the difference between these two, let's take a scenic tour to clear things up.

Here's a little metaphor to make the comparison more digestible. Think of permanent and term life insurance as two paths to owning that dream house you've always wanted. Term life insurance is like leasing an apartment. You sign on the dotted line for a fixed term, like a year, and pay rent throughout that period. As long as you stay current on your rent, you can enjoy all the perks of living in the apartment. But, these perks have an expiry date - they only last as long as your lease. Once the lease is up, you got to move out.

If the thought of your term life insurance expiring and leaving you unprotected gives you the heebie-jeebies, it might be high time to consider permanent life insurance. Using a housing metaphor, permanent life insurance is like buying a house instead of leasing it. With a permanent life insurance policy, you're covered for your entire lifetime, so there's no worry about your coverage ending. As long as you keep up with your premium payments, the policy remains active, and when you bid your final farewell, the benefits are handed over to your beneficiaries.

Term-Life Insurance (The Temporary Lifeline)

Let's face it - death is life's ultimate curveball, and to help handle this harsh reality, loads of people turn to term life insurance, primarily because it doesn't bust the bank. In contrast to permanent life insurance, the term is easier on your wallet because it doesn't stack up any cash value, and it only covers a limited stretch, usually 10, 20, 25, or 30 years.

Steady and Decreasing Term

Level-term life insurance is like having a safety net for a set term, offering a fixed payout no matter when the Grim Reaper decides to pay a visit. If life throws a knuckleball and the policyholder passes away, the beneficiaries get the full benefit from the policy. On the flip side, decreasing term life insurance is more like a sand clock, with the payout shrinking over time. People usually opt for decreasing terms when they've got some pressing financial needs -

like paying off a debt, covering their kids' college fees, or a wedding blowout. A common use for decreasing term life insurance is to whittle down a mortgage balance. Remember, the safety net disappears when the policyholder breathes their last, so make the most of it while the insured is still kicking.

Renewable Term Life

With renewable term life insurance, the policyholder gets to hit the refresh button and renew the policy once the term wraps up. But keep in mind that the renewal sticker price will be steeper than the original term. The premium for the new term is crunched based on the insured's current age and health status.

Convertible Term Life

Some term life insurance policies come with a cool feature — the ability to morph some or all of the term coverage into a permanent life insurance policy. That means you can switch your term life insurance policy to a permanent one, like whole life or universal life insurance. And the best part? Once you flip the switch, you can start reaping the benefits of permanent life insurance pronto.

Peeling back the layers of term life insurance empowers you to make decisions that are in sync with your individual needs and financial picture. By giving the terms, perks, and features offered by insurance companies a thorough once-over, you can choose a policy that aligns with your long-range financial aspirations and provides the coverage you need for the duration you want.

When you're sizing up term life insurance options, don't forget to weigh how long you need coverage, the payout you're shooting for, and any specific financial responsibilities or targets you need to tackle. Give the policy's renewal options, conversion prospects, and additional perks or benefits a close look.

Comparison shopping — getting quotes and understanding policy details from various insurance providers — is a solid strategy, as it helps you spot a good deal and find the most bang-for-your-buck coverage for your budget. Touching base with an insurance guru can clear up any doubts and ensure you're crystal clear on all policy aspects before you commit.

Ultimately, picking the right flavor of term life insurance calls for careful thought about your personal situation, future financial game plan, and the level of protection you want. By doing your homework and picking the brains of experts, you can make an informed choice that offers financial stability and peace of mind for you and your family.

Permanent Life Insurance

Now, with permanent life insurance, you're not just borrowing for a while; you're becoming the bona fide owner. Just like buying a car instead of leasing it, ownership comes with a full suite of benefits, so long as you keep up with the premium payments. It's like paying taxes - you chip in your bit, and the government takes care of you in return. In the same way, regular premium payments to your insurance company ensure financial safety and support for you and your beneficiaries throughout your lifetime and even beyond.

One of the standout perks of permanent life insurance is that the policy's value keeps growing as long as you keep up with the premiums. Although permanent life insurance might come with a heftier price tag than term life insurance, the fact that the policy value increases over time means you and your beneficiaries can gain from it in the long run.

Unlike term life insurance, which often jacks up the cost with each renewal, permanent life insurance allows you to accrue extra assets or benefits without needing additional payments each time. This allows policyholders to tackle evolving financial needs or jump on new opportunities without shelling out more cash.

Now that we've pulled back the curtain on permanent life insurance let's shine a light on the different types of permanent life insurance policies to give you a bird's-eye view of all the options out there.

Permanent Life Insurance Types

Whole Life Insurance

Whole life insurance, often linked with the Infinite Banking Concept (IBC), is like having a friend for life. This pal promises to stick around for as long as you live, guarantees to leave a financial legacy for your loved ones, and diligently stashes away some cash value over time. With steady premium payments, you get to beef up your policy's value and could even use it as a safety net for a loan down the line.

Universal Life Insurance

On the other hand, universal life insurance, another long-term buddy, comes with more flexibility and puts you in the driver's seat. It lets you call the shots on the policy's expiry age and tweak the premium payments to match your financial ambitions. You could also pocket some tax benefits as the policy's value bulks up. With universal life insurance, you can tap into your policy's cash value while keeping yourself covered for the long haul.

Index Universal Life Insurance

Are you looking for long-term benefits and the chance to grow your assets over time? Index universal life insurance could be your answer. This policy ties the cash value to the performance of a specific index, like the stock market. So, when the markets on a roll, your policy's cash value also enjoys the ride. But don't sweat the market dips - your policy is safe from market downturns. With index universal life insurance, you set the terms of the policy, and it leaves a financial gift for your beneficiaries when you're gone.

Other Permanent Life Insurance Options

Joint First-to-Die Life Insurance

This policy is like a two-for-one deal, covering two folks, such as spouses or siblings, under a single policy. If one person bites the dust, the surviving person gets the payout. If life throws a curveball, it's a financial safety net for couples or siblings.

Supplemental Life Insurance

This type of policy is an employee bonus, usually given by employers to take care of their workers' day-to-day needs, like school fees, rent, or utility bills. It could also come with a medical expense cover. If the employee passes away, their family can lean on this policy.

Credit Life Insurance

Credit life insurance safeguards specific debts, like a mortgage, boat loan, or global corporation investment. If you kick the bucket, the policy covers either the entire debt or a chunk of it based on the premium payments. Licensed insurance companies, banks, and loan providers usually offer it.

These are just a handful of permanent life insurance options out there. Picking a policy depends on your unique needs and what you're looking for. Some policies cater to everyday expenses, and others cover specific financial commitments. Make sure you read the fine print and weigh up the benefits of each policy to find the one that's the best fit for you.

3 — Infinite Banking Goal Today

Money can be a scary subject for many people. The thought of what could happen if they run out of money sends shivers down their spine. Losing your job? Your loved one is left in the dark if something happens to you. These are all too real fears.

In today's world, where joblessness is a genuine concern, financial worry is the boogeyman in the room. The what-ifs of finding themselves in a sticky situation haunt many people's thoughts. Yet, despite the uncertainty, folks are always hustling, trying to keep their heads above water. Sadly, many fall into a whirlpool of debt in their attempt to put food on the table. Borrowing money from friends, companies, banks, you name it, and this debt lands them in hot water.

But it doesn't have to be a downward spiral. Many are hunting for ways to whittle down their debts. Still, governments across the globe are making it more challenging by putting the brakes on tax reforms. People are playing the stock market or setting up businesses but dipping into their piggy banks to do so.

Savings are supposed to be the golden egg for retirement, but many end up raiding their nest egg to cover everyday expenses. That's where infinite banking comes to the rescue. With the Infinite Banking Concept (IBC), you can access the money you need without draining your savings. As we've seen, Nelson Nash first whipped up this concept in the 1980s, and it's still a lifeline in today's volatile world.

So, how do you get the ball rolling with IBC? Whether you're up to your neck in debt or on the home stretch to paying it off, planning is vital given the unpredictable nature of our current world. Let's say you're in a cushy job with a monthly salary of $20,000, and your monthly expenses hover between $5,000 and $10,000. You can squirrel away a chunk of your salary to build up a nice little nest egg for retirement.

You can opt to use your assets to snap up an insurance policy, like whole life insurance or a term policy. Both types of policies are great safety nets for your future. If life throws you a curveball and you need money, you can cash out your policy before it matures. But before we get down to the nitty-gritty of infinite banking or whole life insurance, let's discuss the key steps to safeguard your prized assets.

To make sure you don't hit a snag while buying your policy, follow these steps:

Before diving head-first into the Infinite Banking Concept (IBC), you must clearly understand what you hope to achieve through it. Are you looking to build wealth over time to secure a financially stable future for your family or to have easy access to funds for investment purposes? Each goal may require a slightly different approach to how you implement IBC.

When using your life insurance policy as a banking system, consider why and when you might need to take a loan against your policy. Are you hoping to have access to funds for potential investment opportunities, emergency expenses, or supplementing your retirement income? Understanding your 'why' can guide your 'how.'

Consider your long-term financial objectives and how IBC can help you achieve them. Are you hoping to reduce your reliance on traditional banks, to grow wealth that you can pass on to future generations, or to have a safety net for uncertain times? Having a clear vision of your future can guide your present decisions.

Setting clear, realistic goals will help you plan effectively and stay motivated throughout the journey. It's important to remember that IBC is not a get-rich- quick scheme but a strategic tool to build wealth and security over time.

You can effectively implement the Infinite Banking Concept by conducting thorough research, finding a knowledgeable and reliable agent, and understanding your end goals. This strategy could help you create a secure financial future for yourself and your family, offer increased financial independence, and help you navigate uncertain economic times with greater peace of mind.

Understand the End Goal

You're probably asking why I would want to get into infinite banking, right? Well, imagine having your money working for you, even when you need to borrow against it. That's the main idea behind the infinite banking concept, and it can be a game-changer. But before you dive in, you need to ask yourself a few key questions. What are your financial goals? What do you want to achieve long- term? Having a clear picture of where you want to be lets you make better decisions now and set yourself up for a brighter financial future.

Starting with infinite banking can seem daunting, but don't worry; it's not rocket science. You start by setting some money aside and looking into life insurance policies like whole life or term. Do your research, find a solid insurance agent, and get clear about what you want to achieve. With these steps, you can use the infinite banking concept to navigate through life's financial twists and turns with more confidence.

What's more, this isn't about getting into more debt, but quite the opposite. It's about making your money work harder for you. And as you get into the swing of things, it's important to keep checking in on your goals and adjusting your plans as needed. Life has a way of throwing curveballs, but with a solid foundation in infinite banking, you can weather the storms more easily.

Alongside the nitty-gritty of infinite banking, there's also a shift in mindset that comes with it. It's about taking charge of your financial life and being the one who makes the decisions. It's about feeling empowered and being disciplined with your finances, balancing growing your cash value with managing other financial responsibilities.

Remember that infinite banking isn't a magic solution or a way to get rich quickly. It's a long-term strategy that takes time, patience, and commitment. But the payoff can be huge, like building wealth that can benefit your family for generations and achieving financial independence.

As you progress on this journey, feel free to contact professionals like experienced insurance agents or financial advisors. They can offer valuable insights tailored to your unique circumstances and help guide you on your path.

At the end of the day, infinite banking aims to give you the power to shape your financial future, reduce risk, and build wealth over time. By sticking to infinite banking principles and a disciplined mindset, you can lay a solid financial foundation that'll serve you and your loved ones for years to come.

Your journey with infinite banking is unique to you. So embrace the opportunities, navigate the challenges, and learn from your experiences. Stay focused on your goals, adapt to the ever-changing financial landscape, and take pride in the freedom and peace of mind that comes from being in control of your financial destiny.

About IBC and Whole Life Insurance

Nash first introduced the idea of using your insurance policy as a personal banking system. With whole life insurance, you have what's called a cash surrender value, which is the worth of your policy plus bonuses from the insurance company. If you stop your policy, you get this cash value. But, if you keep paying your premiums, this value can increase, leading to a larger payout for your beneficiaries.

What's nice about whole life insurance is that you can borrow money against your policy's cash value while you're still alive, and you can use this money for pretty much anything you want. Given how unpredictable life can be, this flexibility can be a real lifesaver.

Just like insurance companies stepped up during the Great Depression, they're still playing a crucial role in today's uncertain world. By leaning into infinite banking, you can harness the power of your whole life insurance policy to create a solid financial system that provides peace of mind in an unpredictable world.

4— Infinite Banking Structure

When you start with an Infinite Banking Concept (IBC) policy, it can feel like trying to assemble a piece of complex furniture without a manual. But don't worry, it's less complicated than it appears, you just have to understand the flow of the overall concept. So, let's roll up our sleeves and unpack this.

The IBC policy is built on four key elements. Think of these as the four pillars holding up your policy:

1. Expense: This is basically the policy's cost, like the admin fees.
2. Mortality: This is all about the costs linked to the insured's death risk. They work this out based on a lot of stats and calculations.
3. Interest: This is the interest you earn on your policy's cash value. It's like a little money engine that helps your policy grow over time.
4. Inflow: This is just a fancy word for your premium payments, which add to your policy's value.

Then you get policy illustrations. These are like snapshots of your policy's performance.

The Guaranteed Illustration is like a safety net, showing the minimum benefits your policy can offer. It's based on more conservative figures, like lower interest rates and higher mortality rates.

The Current Illustration is a picture of how your policy is performing right now, given the current interest and mortality rates. It includes guaranteed and non- guaranteed rates so that you can see your policy's potential growth and benefits over time.

Now, how do you know if these illustrations are legit? Well, you can use the 80% test. A Certified Public Accountant can work out the future value of your payments based on a conservative return rate, usually around 5%. You're good if this calculated value is at least 80% of the death benefit shown in the illustration. If it's less, the illustration might be too optimistic.

Next up, we have life insurance riders. These are like add-ons to your policy, giving you extra coverage to suit your needs.

Accelerated Death Benefit Rider

Allows you to access some of your death benefits early if you're diagnosed with a severe or chronic illness.

Family Income Benefit Rider

Provides your beneficiaries with a regular income after you pass away instead of a lump sum payment.

Waiver of Premium Rider

Means you don't have to pay your premiums if you become partially or permanently disabled and can't work.

Accidental Death Rider

Gives your beneficiaries an additional payout if you die from an accident.

Guaranteed Insurability Rider

Lets you buy extra coverage without a medical exam or proof of insurability, which is helpful during significant life events like getting married or having a baby.

Adding these riders to your policy can make it a better fit for your unique needs, giving you and your loved ones extra financial security.

Remember, understanding the nuts and bolts of your IBC policy helps you make smarter decisions about your financial future. Having an experienced insurance agent or financial advisor by your side can also help you customize your policy to fit your life and financial goals, bringing you long-term stability and peace of mind.

Non-direct Vs. Direct Recognition Life Insurance

Let's discuss an important topic you need to know when dealing with life insurance — the difference between non-direct recognition and direct recognition. Trust me; it's simpler than it sounds. Different people have different needs, so both options have their perks. But, whole life insurance is usually best for long-term plans. Anyway, let's break it down.

Non-Direct Recognition:

With this type of policy, the insurance company doesn't care if you take out policy loans. If you take out a loan against your policy, your premium will keep growing as if you didn't borrow anything. So, instead of your bonus getting hit because of the loan you took, you'll still receive the full bonus based on the total assets of your policy.

You might think, "Cool, so I get to keep my cake and eat it too. But, what's in it for the insurance guys?" Well, they also win in two ways. First, they get to play around with flexible interest rates, which can increase or decrease based on how the market is doing. The better the market, the bigger the bonus for the insurance folks.

Direct Recognition:

Now, let's flip the script. With a direct recognition policy, the insurance company adjusts the interest rate and cash value based on the loan you take against your policy. For instance, if your whole life policy is worth $200,000 and you take out a loan of $40,000, your bonuses will be calculated on the remaining $160,000.

In this scenario, you're the only one who gets the loan, and it comes with a fixed interest rate. This is good for the insurance company because only one person (you) applies for the loan and has to pay it back. The other benefits of your policy aren't affected, and you still get the full payout of your policy at the promised time.

It's important to understand these differences when considering borrowing against your life insurance policy. It helps you determine how the loan impacts your bonuses and lets you make a decision that's best for your financial needs and goals. It's always a good idea to talk things over with your insurance agent. They can provide some clear insights and advice based on your unique policy and situation.

Choosing between non-direct recognition and direct recognition really depends on what you need, your comfort level with risk, and your long-term financial plans. By weighing these options and working with your insurance agent, you can pick the best policy for your goals, and give yourself the flexibility and benefits you want.

5 — Double Your Cash or Surrender

When you think about life insurance, you probably picture it as a safety net for your family when you're no longer around. But what if I told you that a cash-value life insurance policy could be more like your rich uncle who loves to help out when you're in a bind. Essentially, that's what it is. It's a treasure trove you can tap into throughout your life, depending on how you manage the policy.

Yes, cash-value policies are a bit pricier than term life insurance, but the benefits make the extra cost worth it because you have access to some of that added cost for the policy. It's not just insurance. It's a financial tool that grows with you over time as you make contributions. You can use the cash you've accumulated in the policy to do things like fund your retirement lifestyle, pay for your kid's college tuition, or even invest in a business venture. It's your money, and you can access it when you need it, on your terms.

Like any financial tool, there is a lot to know and understand to get the most out of the policy. It has benefits and downsides. For example, if you opt out too soon, you may have to pay surrender fees, or the death benefit could shrink if you borrow against your policy without paying back the loan.

The question is, do you want to play the long game and potentially double your cash, or cut the cord and surrender your policy? That's why it's so important to have a knowledgeable advisor who can walk you through these details and help you make the best decision. Surrendering your policy is an irreversible action, and it is best to make sure that choice aligns with your financial goals and personal situation.

Reasons for Surrendering a Life Insurance Policy

Now, let's talk about surrendering a life insurance policy. You bought the policy for a reason, right? Well, people also have reasons to surrender a policy. One big reason could be that you need some quick cash. You may have hospital bills to pay or want to buy a home. Surrendering your life insurance policy lets you get your hands on some cash quickly.

Some people let go of their policy for good reason — they no longer need it. Let's say you are the primary income earner for your family and you bought a life insurance policy for peace of mind to ensure your family is taken care of if something catastrophic happens to you. But once your kids grow up and start supporting themselves, you may not need that insurance anymore. You might also choose to surrender your life insurance if it gets too expensive or underperforms.

Cost of Surrendering a Life Insurance Policy

Surrendering a life insurance policy has its costs — literally. You'll have to pay what's called a surrender charge if you terminate the policy before it matures. The exact amount can vary, depending on your policy. If you're considering terminating your life insurance, it's a good idea to discuss it with someone that will help you look at the benefits and costs of surrender.

There's no secondary market for life insurance. So, if you own a policy, there's no easy way to "sell" your surrender option in a free market. That means surrendering the policy is the only way to get value from it. More and more policy owners are surrendering their options because they need cash quickly or because it makes more sense to surrender the policy than to keep it.

When you surrender a life insurance policy, you also lose the benefits of growth from the swings in market conditions. When interest rates are low, the policy may not make sense to keep, but these policies are designed for the long game. There are also times of inflation where interest rates go up and the policy could enjoy significant compounding growth. When you surrender, you lose the benefits of those big waves t h a t come with inflation and higher interest rates.

If you surrender your policy, you can get all the money you've put into it minus any surrender costs. But remember, you'll have to pay taxes on any gains from the policy's cash value. By surrendering your life insurance plan, you're giving up a lot, so only surrender if you have no better alternative.

Surrender Options

Surrendering your policy should be a last resort. If you are struggling with the cost of the premiums, don't just throw in the towel — there are other options. You could lower the face value of the policy, which would then lower the premium. You can also use the cash value to convert the policy to a paid-up status. This way, you can keep some coverage. If you're in a real financial bind, you could use your policy's cash value to pay the premiums for a little while. But be careful not to use up all of your cash value because that could cause your policy to lapse.

There are pros and cons to surrendering a policy. On the pro side, if your policy has a cash or surrender value higher than the surrender charge, you get to keep the difference. But conversely, if you have any charges in arrears, they could eat up all your cash value. You'd then have to pay taxes, and none of your beneficiaries would get the death benefit.

Before you decide to surrender your life insurance policy, it's important to weigh the pros and cons carefully. Look into other options and talk to professionals to make an informed decision. Remember, surrendering should only be on the table when you've thoroughly checked out all other possibilities.

Here's another thing to keep in mind: when you surrender a life insurance policy, you lose the rights that come with it, including the ability to pass on death benefits. You might think you don't need life insurance right now, but remember that your circumstances can change - and they probably will. Our financial needs shift as we move through life, and by surrendering a policy early, you're shutting the door on future possibilities.

New policies often have surrender charges, which can be hefty and reduce the surrender value. There could also be tax implications. If the surrender value exceeds the policy basis, you'll have to pay income tax on the gain. But this might not apply if the life insurance policy is replaced or exchanged during a qualifying transaction. In those cases, any taxable gain from the policy surrender could be deferred.

Options

You might be thinking, "Is surrendering my insurance policy really an option?" It might seem a little unconventional, but don't fret! There are various routes you can take if you're considering a policy surrender. Who knows, one might just be the perfect fit for you.

Here are a few options:

Taking Out a Policy Loan

You can use the money you've built up in your life insurance policy and borrow against it, much like getting a loan with your house as collateral. This way, you still hold onto your policy rights. The interest rate might be a bit steeper than your typical bank loan, but the beauty of it is that you don't necessarily have to pay it back. Any outstanding amount is just deducted from your death benefit or potential surrender value. Bonus, the interest on your loan isn't taxable unless it's for business purposes.

Cash Value Withdrawal

If taking a loan doesn't seem like your cup of tea, there's another way. You can dip into the cash value of your life insurance policy. Unlike a loan, this will reduce your death benefit for good, but at least you won't be worrying about interest payments. Do keep in mind that if you go over your policy's cost basis with your withdrawals, you're going to have to pay taxes on it.

Viatical Settlement

If you've been diagnosed with a terminal illness, this option could be for you. It lets you sell your policy to a viatical settlement provider, essentially a third party. You give up your policy rights, but you get a chunk of cash in return, typically around 40% to 85% of your policy's overall value.

Life Settlement

This is a bit like a viatical settlement, except it's for those who aren't terminally ill. You sell your policy to a third party, and any money you get from the sale is taxed.

Policy Lapse

This happens when you stop paying your premiums. Your insurance provider will use the cash value you've built up to pay out a settlement, and then your policy will eventually lapse unless the cash value is high enough to generate dividends that keep the policy afloat.

Tapping into the Accelerated Death Benefit

You might want to take a good look at your life insurance policy. If it has an accelerated death benefit clause, it could mean you're eligible to receive some of your death benefit early. This could be handy if you need long-term care or are dealing with a chronic illness.

Don't Forget About Taxes

If you decide to surrender your policy, you'll be taxed on any profit you make, just like regular income. To work out your profit, take your policy's cash value and subtract any unearned dividends, surrender charges, and premiums. If you have a policy loan, it gets a bit tricky, but here's the math: Gain = (Cash value + unearned dividends and terminal dividends - surrender charges) + policy loan - basis.

You might be wondering, "But is a life insurance loan a better option?" The short answer is absolutely! If you take out a life insurance loan, you're not saying goodbye to your life insurance. Your insurer lends you the money, using your cash value as a kind of safety net.

In fact, many financial advisors recommend taking out loans against your insurance policy, especially if you're someone who no longer needs the death benefit for your beneficiaries. Maybe you're a retiree with grown, independent children or a widow or widower.

If you're uncomfortable putting your assets, like your house or car, on the line as collateral, then a policy loan could be just the ticket. It's an easier process than getting a loan from a traditional bank or lender. A policy loan could be the way to go if:

You Can't Get A Bank Loan:

Maybe your credit score isn't great, but that won't stop you from getting a life insurance loan. Life insurance companies don't check your credit score; they only check if you have enough cash value in your policy. Plus, it won't impact your credit score since there are no credit-related inquiries.

You Don't Want to Risk Your Assets:

Traditional lenders want collateral like a car or house. If you don't repay the loan, they can take that collateral. With a life insurance policy loan, the worst that can happen is you lose your coverage, which might put a financial burden on your beneficiaries after your death. But that's still better than losing your assets.

You're Able to Repay the Policy Loan:

If your life insurance policy has built up a substantial cash value, repaying the loan should be less of a burden.

You Want Flexible Repayment:

Unlike banks, which expect you to repay loans within a certain time frame and through installments, life insurance policy loans have no set repayment schedule. But, remember, not repaying does have its consequences - namely, the loss of your coverage.

So, as we journey onto the next topic, remember to know your rights and make sure you're making an informed decision. After all, knowledge is power!

6 — Application of the Infinite Banking Concept

You've got a handle on the IBC and all the goodies it offers—think convenience and low risk over old-school banking. Now, let's throw in some real-world examples to make it clearer.

Picture this—you see a sleek Mercedes that you've got to have, but your bank balance says "no way". The traditional saving plan doesn't look promising; it would take ages to stack up that much cash. So, what's a car lover to do? Just keep saving until the dream car is within reach? Nope, that's not the only way!

Enter infinite banking, your dream-come-true solution. But first things first, to kickstart the infinite banking system, you need a life insurance policy. This is the powerhouse behind IBC. Now back to the Mercedes story. With your life insurance policy, you can borrow $25,000 to snag that luxury ride. Once you've got the car keys in hand, you start repaying the loan over 5 years at a 5% interest rate. Here's how it plays out:

You'd fork over $475 monthly. After five years, you'd have paid back the borrowed sum plus interest, totaling $28,000. The awesome part is you're not just repaying yourself; you're also earning interest. Cool, huh?

It gets even better. While you're taking care of the loan and interest, your cash value is busy growing due to compound interest. So, you're essentially doubling up in one place. After five years, you can even get another car and repay yourself the same way.

Infinite banking is not a new kid on the block. It's been around for decades, thanks to Nelson Nash. This system basically kicks middlemen like commercial banks and traditional creditors to the curb, along with their lengthy loan processes. As an insured person, you just need to pay a chunky premium and wait for the policy to mature. Payments can be monthly or yearly. The beauty of infinite banking is it's straightforward and doesn't eat up much time.

With infinite banking, you're the boss. You can reach into your funds for big- ticket purchases like that Mercedes, without leaning on traditional banks. You're funding yourself, repaying yourself, and earning interest while your cash value keeps rising.

Infinite banking sounds like magic but remember: only borrow if you're sure you can handle the financial commitment. The plus side is the cash you use and repay is all yours. Your cash/surrender value acts as loan collateral, but not paying back can mess up your life insurance policy.

One of the big wins with infinite banking is it keeps its value even during tough economic times or when the market is tanking. It doesn't dance to the tune of market trends, so it's a safe financial choice. It's highly liquid and insurance companies give it the thumbs up as collateral for policy loans when needed. Traditional banks and creditors, on the other hand, often want tons of financial and personal info to approve a loan, which can drag out the process. In urgent situations, you just don't have that kind of time.

To get the most out of the infinite banking system, keep up with the policy terms.

Economic Crises and Infinite Banking

The world has seen its fair share of financial blowouts, like the 2008/09 economic crisis, which hit America hard. One in five employees lost their jobs, white-collar opportunities became rare, and disability claims shot up as job hunting got tougher. It was a grim time that left a lasting mark on people's dreams of owning homes, starting families, and buying cars.

The government stepped in with bailouts to steady the economy and fend off more bankruptcies. Unfortunately, the bigwigs at the banks and financial institutions that sparked the crisis got off scot-free due to the complexities of taking on such huge entities. That's where infinite banking comes in, offering a lifeline in a harsh financial landscape.

Imagine being back in 2008 during the economic meltdown. Your company's downsizing and you get an email saying your job's been axed. You're thrown into a panic and share the bad news with your wife. She's staying positive, but you're cool as a cucumber because you've got a plan.

Your calmness comes from your foresight in getting life insurance with a 20-year policy and a 7-year premium payment term. You bought the policy when the economy was still okay, but things were starting to shake up. You were 34 when you signed up for this package. By the time you hit 41 and have been paying premiums for 7 years, you've forked over a total of $419,900 (that's $4,999 monthly). Now, with the financial crisis raging and bills piling up, you've got only one move: contact your insurance company and borrow some cash, say $419,000 or less. The policy is backed by corporate and government securities, so the real amount you can tap into is even higher. The loan gets processed and issued swiftly.

What makes you even happier is that the loan isn't taxed, and you can use it for other investments. During a financial crisis, homeowners and investors may have to sell off their assets, which means you can swoop in and buy up properties at bargain prices. For instance, you can pick up two or three properties in the neighborhood or invest in a city-center apartment. You've got lots of options for smart investments. Just remember the golden rule: "buy low, sell high."

The great thing about life insurance coverage is it's not affected by market ups and downs, so it keeps a steady net value. This stability offers a quick fix during uncertain and financially challenging times.

Infinite banking is a sure bet for working professionals. But if you're a peer-to- peer lender, stock market specialist, angel investor, venture capitalist, or day trader, infinite banking might not jive with your goals. It's not a get-rich-quick scheme, and it doesn't bank on a booming stock market to make a profit. It's designed for people who want to build wealth over time.

Infinite banking isn't a one-size-fits-all solution. It calls for a long-term outlook and dedication to growing wealth. It provides stability and protection against economic downturns, making it a solid tool for anyone seeking financial security and growth.

To wrap up, infinite banking gives you a way to tap into your life insurance policy for immediate financial needs while still growing your cash value. It offers flexibility, liquidity, and control over your financial destiny. By understanding the dos and don'ts of infinite banking, you can reap the benefits and sail through economic ups and downs with confidence.

Infinite Banking Concept—A Safe Financial Harbor

The IBC is a financial haven for many reasons, and the wise investment strategy of insurance companies is one of them. About 90% of an insurance company's portfolio is tied up in investment-grade properties and fixed income.

Insurance companies are smart investors, putting their money in long-term corporate bonds with investment-grade ratings. When inflation and interest rates go up, these bonds dish out higher returns and attractive dividends. This means during inflation; policyholders can earn decent interest on their investments.

On top of that, the bonds insurance companies hold are spread across various industries and companies, ensuring a secure and risk-averse investment approach. Unlike direct investments in real estate or other volatile assets, policy investments aren't exposed to market risks. Even during major economic downturns like the 2008 economic crisis or the Great Depression, dividend payments from the policy remain steady. This stability gives policyholders peace of mind and consistent returns on their investment, regardless of what's happening in the market.

Infinite banking is a safe financial haven. It safeguards policyholders' assets and provides a reliable income stream even in tough times. Yes, you have to pay high premiums to get into infinite banking, but this solution can be a lifesaver in difficult situations.

In short, insurance companies' investment strategy of sticking to high-quality assets like investment-grade properties and fixed income contributes to the safety and stability of infinite banking. Policyholders can count on their investments to yield consistent returns and offer financial security, no matter what the market or economy is doing. Infinite banking is a dependable and secure financial solution for those seeking long-term stability and growth.

7— Cash Value

Alright, we've been talking about Infinite Banking Concept (IBC) for a while now, but there's a really important bit I want to dig into deeper: cash value. Let's start with what it means.

What's Cash Value, Anyway?

Think of cash value as your secret stash. It's part of your life insurance policy that builds up over time, and it's also known as surrender value or cash surrender. It's basically the insurance company promising to give you back some of the money you've paid into your policy if you decide to throw in the towel early. The catch? You've got to buy life insurance and then give up any future benefits from the policy. The good news is you can take that cash and roll it back into the policy to keep things going. But how does that work?

How Cash Value Works

Imagine you have a piggy bank that's tied to a life insurance policy. The piggy bank represents the "cash value" part of your policy.

Every time you pay your life insurance premium, a portion goes into this piggy bank. This is like adding money to your piggy bank every time you pay your premium. Over time, this piggy bank grows and earns interest, similar to how your savings might grow if you kept putting money in a savings account at a bank.

The money in this piggy bank can be used in several ways. You can:

Borrow

Just like you might dip into your savings for emergencies or big purchases, you can also borrow from your cash value. The key point here is that it's a loan, so you'll have to pay it back with interest. However, if you don't repay it, the loan amount will be deducted from the death benefit when you pass away.

Withdraw

In some cases, you can take some money out of your piggy bank (cash value) without having to pay it back. This will, however, reduce your death benefit, which is the amount your beneficiaries receive when you pass away.

Pay Your Premiums

If your piggy bank (cash value) grows enough, you can use it to pay your life insurance premiums.

Surrender the Policy for Cash

If you decide that you no longer want the life insurance policy, you can "surrender" (or cancel) it. You'll then receive the money that's in your piggy bank, but your life insurance coverage will end.

The life insurance part of the policy works just like any life insurance policy. If you pass away while the policy is in effect, your beneficiaries receive a payout, known as a death benefit. The amount they receive is the face value of the policy minus any outstanding loans you've taken from the cash value, if any.

Remember, while this piggy bank feature can be very useful, cash-value life insurance policies can be more expensive than term life insurance policies, which don't have a cash-value component. They just provide a death benefit for a specific period or "term." It's essential to weigh the costs and benefits when deciding on the type of life insurance that's best for you.

Cash Value in Action

Imagine you've got a policy worth $30,000, and you've never borrowed or withdrawn from it. Your cash value would be $3,000. If something happens to you, your family gets the full $30,000. So, your cash value acts as a nice little nest egg, bumping up your total assets to about $15,000.

If you're still scratching your head about how cash value can boost your investment, let's weigh up the pros and cons.

Cash Value

The Good, The Bad, and The Ugly When it comes to life insurance, you can't just jump in without doing your homework.

Pros of Cash Value

Think of cash value as a promise from your insurance company. It's a living benefit that lets you build up your assets. It's also there for you in a pinch - you can borrow against your life insurance if you need to. Everyone wins with cash value - you, your family, and the insurance company. Even if you decide to cancel your policy or the insurance company scales back your benefits, you'll still get your cash value. And you can get your hands on it by making a withdrawal or a partial surrender.

Cons of Cash Value

But, like anything, there's a flip side. If you make a withdrawal or partial surrender, you won't get the death benefit after you're gone.

And you won't have to pay any tax until you make a withdrawal. After that, you're on the hook for the full amount. Some policies let you make withdrawals for life, while others cap the amount you can take out, like $700, for example.

Apart from weighing the pros and cons, there's one more thing you need to think about. As your cash value grows, you could take that money and invest it elsewhere. Here's how.

Your Own Personal Banking System

Cash Flow Banking

Imagine being your own banker. That's the idea behind cash flow banking. It lets you earn money from your investments. The profit comes from the cash your assets generate. But you can only get in on this if you have whole life insurance and are willing to pay extra premiums for a more secure and beneficial investment.

Why Cash Flow Matters to Investors

Doing a cash flow analysis can help investors judge how their investments are doing. It gives them a peek into how much money the business is making and helps them plan for future ventures and other things that could help the business. It's like having a roadmap for where to put your investment dollars.

For example, let's say there's a business that's one year old and is doing pretty well but wants to bring in investors to help it grow. Investors would take a hard look at the business, especially its finances. If the business had a great first year but didn't meet the investor's financial expectations, the investor might have second thoughts. That's where cash flow analysis comes in. It gives the investor a clear picture of the business's finances, helping them decide whether to invest or lend a helping hand. It's also crucial when applying for a loan from a bank, as it shows whether the business is financially sound.

Understanding cash value is key when it comes to life insurance policies. It gives policyholders a lifeline in tough times and can be a powerful financial tool. Cash flow banking and cash flow analysis offer policyholders a way to pump up their investments and make informed decisions about their financial strategies. And remember, it's crucial to do your research and weigh the pros and cons before investing in any insurance product, especially life insurance.

And finally, here's a biggie: why do investors demand a cash flow statement?

When a business is on the hunt for investors, they need to hand over the goods about their finances. Looking at a cash flow analysis report can help investors understand the financial health of the business. They can also see where they might want to put their money.

For instance, say a business makes sports equipment. Investors would look at the cash flow to decide which product to invest in. If the business is raking in cash from soccer equipment, investors would probably want to put their money there.

The report should also highlight other important areas to give investors a full picture of the company's financial health and its profitable areas. These areas include:

Investment Cash Flow

How much cash the business's investments are generating? Operating cash flow — the cost of running the business, including inflows and outflows. Financing cash flow - how the business handles its financial relationships with other investors and creditors. Net cash flow - the total of all of the above, showing the overall cash flow.

By thoroughly researching everything, investors can make sure they're putting their money in the right place.

Before you share a business plan with an investor, you've got to have a strategy to grow your wealth. Wealth strategies are key to boosting revenue growth and making smart investment decisions. They help people spot promising investment opportunities to grow their businesses. Here are a few strategies to consider:

Syndication

Teaming up with seasoned investors for a particular business venture. Turnkey - buying properties, sprucing them up, and then selling them. Mortgage Notes - buying mortgages from banks at affordable prices.

By using these wealth strategies, you can uncover different ways to make money and get the most out of your investments. Remember, it's crucial to do your homework and understand each strategy before you decide which one suits your financial goals and risk tolerance.

8— Is Infinite Banking a Reality?

You've got the hang of this infinite banking concept, right? It's all about treating your life insurance policy as your very own personal banking system. The basic idea is that you are borrowing against your own asset. The cash value is the asset and the more premiums you pay, the more your asset grows.

The best part is that you get to decide how to spend your money. You could use it to buy a car, pay your kids' college tuition, or even cover medical expenses. And guess what? No matter how much you borrow, your life insurance benefits remain untouched. Pretty cool, huh?

Now, infinite banking seems like a godsend for those who truly understand it. It's there for you in times of need. But, like with any good thing, there are doubters. Some folks see it as a sneaky ploy by insurance companies. Others think it's an outdated idea that can't possibly work in today's world. Honestly, people's opinions on infinite banking usually come down to their personal experiences.

But here's the thing - the infinite banking concept isn't exactly new. It's actually been around for quite a while and helped people out during tough times, like the Great Depression. So, it's proven its worth over a very long time.

So, the million-dollar question: Does infinite banking really work? Before we jump to conclusions, let's take a look at some real-life examples of people and companies that have benefited from these policies.

J.C. Penney: Back in the 1930s, during the Great Depression, Penney dipped into his whole life insurance policy to keep his business afloat. He bought inventory, paid his workers - the whole deal.

Ray Kroc: When Ray was struggling to expand McDonald's in the 1960s, he used his life insurance policy to secure a loan, helping him cover salaries and invest in marketing. Just look at where McDonald's is today.

Walt Disney: Even Walt benefited from the infinite banking concept. Banks turned him down when he had the idea for Disneyland. So, what did he do? He leveraged the cash value of his life insurance policy to bring his dream to life.

Doris Christopher: Doris borrowed $3,000 against her life insurance policy to start her venture, Pampered Chef. Her business bloomed and later sold for a whopping $900 million in 2002.

Jim Harbaugh: Jim, the head soccer coach at the University of Michigan, used a $14 million life insurance policy in his contract. If he needs to, he can take out policy loans or make tax-free withdrawals. If he passes away, the university gets the initial $14 million back from the death benefit.

The stories of J.C. Penney, Ray Kroc, Walt Disney, and others show that infinite banking can and does work. Yes, it requires discipline and smart financial choices. If you don't repay your loans, you could face a decrease in policy benefits or penalties. And, of course, your cash value is tied to your specific life insurance policy, which could limit your options for other insurance coverage.

But when used wisely, infinite banking can offer financial security and a solid platform for other investments. It's a powerful tool that puts you in control of your financial life. How effective it is really depends on how you use it. And as the success stories show, it can be a game-changer in achieving financial goals and building wealth over time.

9 — Final Word

As we close the pages of "The Infinite Money Tree," we find ourselves in possession of a profound financial truth that has the potential to redefine our relationship with money. We've unearthed the secret of infinite banking, a seed we can plant today, allowing the sturdy roots of financial security to grow deep into the fertile soil of time.

It's disheartening to witness the money missteps that many of us make, from spending recklessly to incurring burdensome debts and making hasty investment decisions. Yet, the reassuring message resonating from this book is that there's another path - a path of financial wisdom, self-reliance, and steady growth.

Money is not merely a tool to meet our immediate needs or satisfy our fleeting whims. It's a seed with infinite potential that, when planted wisely in the fertile ground of infinite banking, can grow into a robust money tree, offering shade from the harsh sun of economic uncertainty and bearing fruits of wealth to sustain us in our future years.

The secret garden of whole life insurance has been the sanctuary for banks, successful entrepreneurs, and corporations for over a century, empowering them to withstand some of the most challenging economic storms. And yet, this life- changing financial tool remains shrouded in obscurity and misunderstanding among the masses. This is a call to change that narrative.

Remember, whole life insurance isn't just about protecting your loved ones after you're gone, it's about seizing control of your financial destiny while you're still here. It's about stepping off the roller coaster of financial uncertainty and stepping onto the ascending escalator of predictable and reliable growth.

As the inspiring tales of financial transformation shared in this book have shown us, infinite banking is not an elusive dream but a tangible reality. You too can become a part of this narrative, cultivating your own infinite money tree and reaping its rich harvest.

So, take this seed of knowledge and plant it in the fertile soil of action. Nurture it with patience and discipline, and watch as it transforms your financial landscape. Because in your hands lies the power to grow your very own infinite money tree. Will you take that first step towards planting it? Your future self is counting on you.

Curious? Want more information? Ready to get started?

As you journey forward, armed with the insights from "The Infinite Money Tree," know that you are not alone. While the concept of infinite banking may be new and potentially overwhelming to you, I am here to guide you on this exciting financial expedition.

If you find yourself curious, inspired, or simply desiring to understand more about the infinite banking concept and its transformative potential for your financial situation, I invite you to reach out to me directly. I am more than willing to walk with you, illuminating the path and helping you tailor these strategies to your unique circumstances.

This could be the turning point, the moment you decide to plant your own money tree, destined to flourish under the guidance of time and disciplined care. I'm here to help you ensure its growth, providing resources and insights gleaned from years of studying and applying the principles of infinite banking.

Your financial liberation, your journey towards a wealthier, more secure future, starts with a simple step. Reach out to me, let's unravel the intricacies of infinite banking together, and let's make that infinite money tree a reality in your life.

Resources

- s3.amazonaws.com/Greatest-HIts/Why+IBC+Works.pdf
- s3.amazonaws.com/Greatest-HIts/IBC's+Role+in+the+Sound+Money+Solution.pdf
- www.policyholder.gov.in/uploads/CEDocuments/Life%20Insurance%20 Handbook.pdf
- paradigmlife.net/blog/5-businesses-saved-cash-value-life-insurance/
- infinitebanking.org/how-to-weather-the-coming-financial-storms/
- blobby.wsimg.com/go/436a5d1b-2bb2-4311-a1ff-3f0e155e721d/downloads/Becoming-Your-Own-Banker%20eBOOK.pdf
- wealthnation.io/blog/a-comprehensive-guide-to-infinite-banking/
- s3.amazonaws.com/IBC-BankNotes/BankNotes+Mar+2022.pdf
- lifesuccesslegacy.com/wp-content/uploads/Infinite-Banking-How-It-Works_FINAL.pdf
- www.investopedia.com/terms/w/wholelife.asp
- bankingtruths.com/awr-famous-entrepreneurs-whole-life-insurance- bank/
- eml.berkeley.edu/~cromer/Reprints/great_depression.pdf
- www.youtube.com/watch?v=7xGv9_WNtmg
- unctad.org/system/files/official-document/gdsmdp20101_en.pdf
- www.nber.org/system/files/working_papers/w26908/w26908.pdf

NOTES

www.ingramcontent.com/pod-product-compliance
Lightning Source LLC
Chambersburg PA
CBHW072133070526
44585CB00016B/1661